T0198966

BUZZY

My Adventurous Short Life

By Robert "Buzzy" Sweet

Illustrated by Sue Sweet Van Hook

Balboa Press books may be ordered through booksellers or by contacting:

Balboa Press
A Division of Hay House
1663 Liberty Drive
Bloomington, IN 47403
www.balboapress.com
844-682-1282

Because of the dynamic nature of the Internet, any web addresses or links contained in this book may have changed since publication and may no longer be valid. The views expressed in this work are solely those of the author and do not necessarily reflect the views of the publisher, and the publisher hereby disclaims any responsibility for them.

Cover Design: By Tom Sweet
Cover Photo: Last Summer, 1956

ISBN: 978-1-9822-7852-6 (sc)
ISBN: 978-1-9822-7876-2 (e)

Library of Congress Control Number: 2022900427

Print information available on the last page.

Balboa Press rev. date: 02/04/2022

BALBOA.PRESS

Dedication

To all the families who have lost children.

To my brother Buzzy, who lived fully until he died suddenly.

Finding your autobiography has brought immeasurable healing to the family.

Foreword

This is a unique true story written by my brother Buzzy, as an autobiography assignment at age 13, two weeks before he died unexpectedly from acute childhood leukemia in 1957. I have illustrated the text in a manner to evoke the simple creative joy of what a young boy's adventurous life was like before there were digital devices. The story also serves to honor all children who have lost their lives too soon and to help siblings and parents of these children focus on celebrating the short and rich lives of their loved ones. Additionally, my intention is to share the joy of unlimited exploration out of doors that Buzzy experienced in four northeastern states. He was fortunate to spend his summers with our grandparents on the island of North Haven in Penobscot Bay, Maine. I too had these same opportunities a decade later. What comes through in the telling of his life is reverence for his family and friendships, respect for his teachers and classmates, and his humor. [The last names of the other children outside the family have been changed to protect their identity, with the exception of Andy Wuskell, who is alive as of this publication, and who has granted permission to use his name].

I was born June 15, 1943, about 12 o'clock.

The hospital was Waterbury Hospital in Conn.

My parents had wanted a girl, after 2 boys, but they had to be satisfied

with what they got.

My mother said that I weighed about 9 lb. 4 oz.

My mother must have had a lot of fun totin' me around with her.

At the time I was born,

we were living at Durham Ave. in Naugatuck, Connecticut.

Even though my father had wanted a girl,

he had me playing with a basketball at about 5 or 6 months.

When I was 1 yr. old

I took a trip across Long Island Sound on my grandfather's boat.

He had a nice boat that slept 5 or 6 people.

In the summer we went to Pleasantville where my grandfather lived. In the back

yard there was a steep cliff.

At the bottom were some railroad tracks.

I used to sit and watch the trains go by.

Once my oldest brother, Pete, put a penny

on the railroad track.

We went to get the penny after a train

went by.

The penny was twice the size

and Abraham Lincoln had an awfully

funny look on his face.

When I turned three

my grandfather bought a house in North Haven, Maine.

North Haven Island is in Penobscot Bay.

When we went up there, I was scared going across the bay on a ferry.

Also, one day when I was only three my brother wanted to take me for a ride in

a wagon. He put me in back and pulled me up a nice steep hill. We got to the top

and turned the wagon around. My brother got in front and we started down.

Boy! Was I scared.

When we got near the bottom my brother somehow lost control of the steering. We went headfirst into a telephone pole. My brother got a nasty cut on his knee and scraped his leg. I was lucky and only got a scraped elbow.

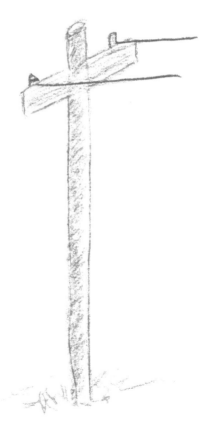

My brother, Jim, still has a scar on his knee.

When we got home my mother was scared stiff.

Neither of us was too badly hurt,

but she wanted to rush us to the hospital.

The next thing I can remember is when I was 4 years old.

It was the summer when I was sick.

My grandfather bought a boat and named it the "Buzzy", after me.

One day they went to town and left me in the house. Mr. Crockett who is the main

milk and dairy man on the island had some cows fenced in on Crabtree Point,

which is where we live. Well, while I was alone, I took a nap.

When I woke up there were cows on our front and back lawns

and down on the beach.

I was scared that they would break in the house, but they didn't.

When my grandparents, my parents, and brothers came back in the boat they

wondered what all the people were doing on the beach and if anything had happened

to me. They got an awful surprise when they saw cows walking all over the beach.

When I was 2 our family moved from Naugatuck to Hartford, Conn. Hartford is the capital of Connecticut. In Hartford we lived at 188 Warrenton Ave.

When we were introduced to the people who lived in back of us, we found that there was a boy exactly my age, within 1 month. His name was Andy Wuskell.

He and his brother, John, who was 2 years older, were my best friends and stayed my best friends until now, and still are. We used to play together all the time.

Once we made a giant slingshot out of an old inner tube.

We shot balloons filled with water at people we didn't like.

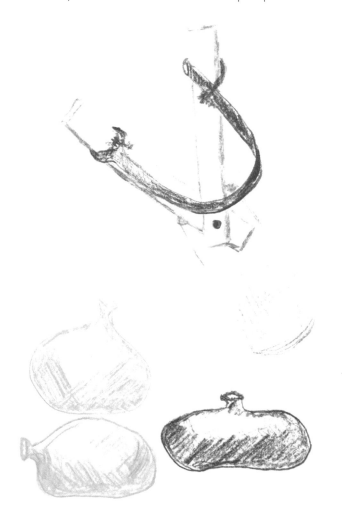

Later we made another slingshot and had wars.

We used to make airplanes and boats in Johnny and Andy's cellar.

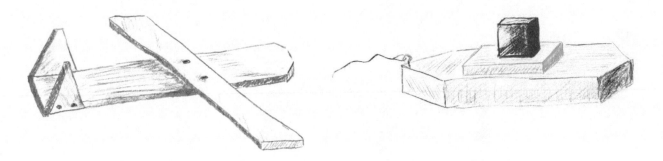

We made bunk beds and slept in the crafts that we made.

The Wuskells had a little recreation room that we had pillow fights in.

In this room they also had a bar with some empty bottles. We filled the bottles with water and played bar. Down in the Wuskell's cellar we set up a good bowling alley.

Mr. Walters, whom we called Uncle Walter, set up a garden each year. His garden stakes made wonderful spears. We didn't want to hurt anybody with the spears, so we tied a piece of sheet around some cotton to make it padded like so:

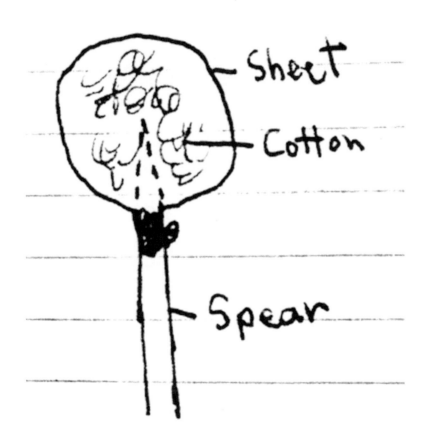

When I was 5 or 6 yrs. old, we made a swing that was able to go very high because we put a lot of rope from the swing to the apple tree.

We used to swing as high as we could and then jump off.

That summer we went up to North Haven for our vacation.

My grandfather had built a shop and bought a lot of tools. We made knives, boats and bird houses.

We went lobstering almost every morning.

When you lobster, you have a buoy that you pick up, a bottle to keep the warp, which is rope, more warp, and the lobster trap.

One day my grandfather and I were out lobstering in our rubber raft. The rubber raft is a navy surplus one. The sides are blown up with air, but the sides are not very strong.

Soon we were almost finished lobstering, but we had to haul one more trap.

When, we hauled that trap the corner of it punctured a hole in the rubber side.

My grandfather and I swam ashore and my two brothers, who were on the

shore, swam out and salvaged anything that was afloat.

When I was four I went to nursery school.

I was one of the best readers in my class.

The teachers wanted me to go to first grade in

this school too, but I went to East school

with my friends.

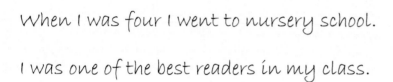

So, when I was five I went to kindergarten.

We had two kindergarten teachers. The first one, Mrs Keeler, had to leave us in the middle of the year. Our second teacher was Miss Braheny.

We had to bring little rugs to school to take our naps on.

I remember Andy Wuskell and I used to roll marbles to each other while everyone else was resting.

Miss Braheny didn't usually catch us, but when she did we had to wash the blackboards.

When we washed the blackboards
we didn't do a good job so we
wouldn't have to do it again.

My first grade teacher was Miss Peterson.

Andy and I were together again. We had recess every day around 10 o'clock.

One day when we were out at recess I had to go back in and get a whistle for our teacher. As soon as I got in the room there was fire alarm.

Everyone thought it was just a practice drill until the fire engines came whipping around the corner.

They ran in the school but couldn't find a fire anywhere.

Then our principal, Mr. Boswell, spotted a broken fire alarm box right outside our classroom.

Everybody said that I accidentally broke it. But I will still swear on any bible that I didn't.

In second grade Andy was not in my class.

He was in Miss Rennig's.

Wuskell and I walked home together

for 6 ½ years straight.

One day while I was alone I decided to bake a cake.

I went to the cupboard and took out vinegar, flour, yeast, turnips, salt and pepper, sugar and coffee grinds. I put this all in a cookie sheet and stuck it in the broiler.

That yeast sure worked awfully good. When my mother came home, I asked her to take my nice cake out of the broiler.

Boy oh boy, what a beautiful mess.

It took my mother 2 days to clean out the oven.

I gave a piece of my cake to our dog.

He went outside and vomited,

but I think it would have been a good cake.

In third grade we had a teacher that would let us get away with murder. She taught 3rd and 4th combined.

Every once-in-a-while she would let me do 4th grade work.

Every day at recess we would have fights. There were two gangs. Bob led one and Andy and I the other.

We won most of the fights even though the other team was a year older than us.

We had a lot of fun in the winter...

...even though I had to write a perfect letter

to the bus company telling them I was sorry

I hit one of their buses with a snowball.

Just before the winter, we made an underground fort.

It was 6 ft long, 5 feet high and 4 or 5 ft wide. We placed beams over the top of the hole.

Then we put plywood over that.

On top of the plywood we put dirt, grass and a little bush.

We had candles for light and heat. We had a smokestack going out of the roof into the bush.

Our fort was perfectly camouflaged. People walked over our heads and didn't even know we were there.

That summer we went to Maine again.

My two brothers and I built a tree fort.

The fort was about 45 feet from the ground.

From this fort you can see land

14 and 15 miles away.

Another event this summer was cows on our property. One morning we woke up to the sweet bellowing of a full-grown cow. The cows were awful pests. Every morning they woke us about 5 o'clock.

Once our dog, Sandy, got filthy from rolling in cow flops. We went to the house and filled a great big tub full of water. My brothers and I went down to get our dog and when we came back there was about 4 or 5 cows around the tub drinking to their hearts content.

We tried to scare them away, but they were thirsty, and they wouldn't be scared or budge.

In fourth grade my teacher was Miss Noyes.

We had to be good because the room was opposite the principal's office.

The principal used to go out with his secretary sometimes.

He would take me out of class to answer any phone call that came for him.

Andy was in Miss Noyes's room also. In back of our school there were some woods and a stream.

We used to see who could make it over wide parts of the stream.

Andy and I almost always made it but Haven Belcher fell in twice.

When Haven fell in, he had to go to the principal's office and boy did he get heck for going where we weren't supposed to go.

My fifth-grade teacher was Mr. Kleinman. He was my first man teacher. He was a nice one though. My friend, Andy, was not in my room this time. My best friend in this room turned out to be Johnny Wickfield. He came from a different school. We both did experiments with his chemistry set.

We made an explosive that stunk out any and I mean any room within five minutes. We used sulphuric acid, potassium nitrate, powdered magnesium and a match head. We lit one of these off in Johnny's cellar and his mother who was on the 2nd floor smelled it coming all the way from the basement. We didn't play with the chemistry set for about another week.

That summer we went to North Haven for our vacation.

When we got there, we found out that our grandmother and grandfather had tamed

a little chipmunk to come out

of the woods and eat right out

of your hand.

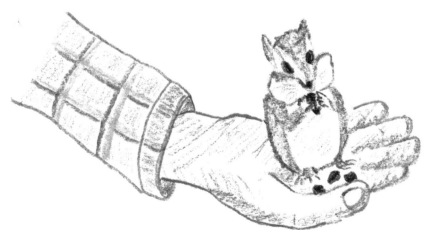

During the course of the summer we made an aqua plane

to tow behind my grandfather's boat.

We went aquaplaning nearly every day

While I was in fifth grade the town was building a new million-dollar elementary

school that we were going to go to the next year.

When I got back from my summer vacation we went to the new school. My sixth grade teacher was Mr. Costello (no relation to Lou Costello of the Abbott & Costello team). He was a real nice teacher. We had a basketball team that was undefeated.

The first string was Mallory, Athens, Calligan, Keenan and Andy Wuskell and I took turns. We played almost every Saturday.

We played inter-mural games, Tuesday and Thursday also.

In our classroom we had a microscope.

We put a drop of water out of the aquarium on it and watched the cells moving.

George Chapman and I came in early to take the chairs down off the desk and we

fooled around with the microscope.

In the middle of the year we moved from West Hartford, Connecticut to Abington Penna. It was April to be exact.

My teacher at this school was Mr. Freeman. The name of the school was Highland.

The school is about a block from my new house.

Some of my friends in Abington are John Duncan, Steve Downton, John Arnot, Miles Truman, Leonard Smulton, and Dave Grayson.

We had a lot of parties that year. I had one myself.

That summer we went to Maine again.

We went lobstering, fishing,

swimming and aqua-planing.

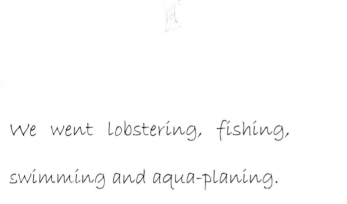

We also worked in my grandfather's shop making bird houses, knives, boats, etc.

This year I am going to Abington Jr. High School. I am in roster #35.

My homeroom teacher is Miss Hand.

My teachers are as follows:

- Social Studies – Miss Hand

- Science – Mr. Willoughby

- English – Mrs. Sutton

- Math – Mr. Berkes

- Hygiene - Mr. Garvin

- Gym - Mr. Garvin

- Music - Mr. Crouthamel

- Art - Mr. Olsen

- Shop - Mr. Schlegel

I was on our school football team playing left tackle. We were undefeated this year. Our hardest game was the last one against Bala Cynwood. We won that by a safety made by Gordon Purshing which gave us the 2 to 0 victory.

I am going out for the seventh-grade basketball team. We have had several practices already. I hope that we will play some inter-mural games. We are now learning the fundamentals.

This is my life until now.

Robert David Sweet

"Buzzy"

June 15, 1943 – January 26, 1957

Junior ★ Star

VOL. 9, NO. 3   JUNIOR STAR   FEBRUARY 22, 1957

Take A Bow

Twenty members of the Service Club received their awards as qualified projectionists in the assembly on January 23. Certificates were awarded to Fred Bartz, Robert Epstein, Richard Fidler, Craig Garnett, Francis Gibbons, Donald Gilchrist, Jack Boeve, Charles Hill, Howard Johnson, Ross Kerr, John Kister, Edmund Salmanson, Harry Smith, Edward Whyte, John Stolfi, Harry McCully, Martin Dodson, James Randall, and Joseph Emsley.

To get this award the boys had to completely operate the audio equipment and 2 slide and 2 motion picture projectors. Now that they have proven their abilities they will be able to operate the equipment in classrooms when the teacher requires assistance.

The boys who have receved their award will be able to go on to Advanced Projectionists. For this they will have to be able to operate all the apparatus except the stage equipment.

It is of value to the boys in that it gives them a feeling of responsibility and achievement, but also satisfies the boy's natural tendency to want to operate mechanical equipment.

In room fifteen there is a chart showing who is qualified to operate a certain piece of equipment.

The officers of the Service Aids Club are Edward Whyte as President and Richard Fidler as vice president.

Treasure Hunt

On Wednesday, February 6, in assembly Miss Davis and homeroom 8-5 gave a quiz program based on the television show "Treasure Hunt." Janet Wunderlich started it off by reading the Bible. Gene Smith was the announcer. Stanley Butler, the master of ceremonies, then started the quiz. The lucky contestants were Miles Truesdell, Carol Archer, Miss Lamont, Mrs. Ricci, Earl Fortenberry, Robin Spence, Fred Groth, Phyllis Ziegler, Judy Jumper, Ralph Olivier.

Library Lingo

Out of a good book to read? Mrs. Fretz and all those who have read them recommend for girls:

"Ramona"
"The Trembling Years"
"Trish"
"A Girl Called Hank"
"Hi! Teacher"
"Green Peace"
"Jane Eyre"
"Showboat Summer"
"Practically Seventeen"

For boys:

"T-Model Tommy"
"Flamingo Feathers"
"Second Try"
"The Star Seekers"
"Danger Dinosaurs"
"Copperhead Hollow"
"Temagami Guide"

All these books can be found in our library at Abington Jr.

HuntingdonDefeats Philip's Boys

On Friday, February 8, 1957, Abington played Huntingdon in basketball at Huntingdon and lost both games. Both teams fought hard but Huntingdon still came out on top with a score of 34-16 in the first game and 34-8 in the second game. Both teams had an equal amount of support from the stands since most of the girls' basketball team walked over to support the boys' team along with a few other rooters.

Robert D. Sweet Dies of Leukemia

Robert David Sweet, son of Mr. and Mrs. Richard B. Sweet of Abington, succumbed January 26, 1957, in the Abington Memorial Hospital. Death was attributed to acute leukemia. Bob, a four-letter athlete at Abington Junior High School, played on the varsity teams in football, basketball, wrestling and track. He was an excellent student and had been elected to the National Honor Society.

A Different Perspective

The myriad of days is done,
They vanished with the
   setting sun.
The prize so highly
   sought is gone—
Instead, a crown of life is won.
So much of life untasted,
So much of world unseen,
So much of youth seems wasted
When death comes to the keen.
Such intellect unmeasured,
Potential unreleased—
His happy smile has vanished,
His family's joys decreased.

We ask the age-old question;
Why death came for the lad.
Why does God take the
   good ones
And leave to earth the bad?
But think, my friends,
   of Robert—
That he is gone above
To live with Him in Heaven
Made whole again by love.

          Helen Geisler

Honor Roll

It looks like we're getting smarter as the year progresses because now there are 22 on the honor roll. Their names are posted in the hall in case you lose this paper. The lucky ones are in 7th grade, Judy Adams, Charles Bonos, Charles Deemer, Barbara Lynne Hartmaire, Susan Leach, John LeRoy, Patricia Manning, Eric Price, Susan Taft, Jean Van Zandt, James Parris. In 8th grade they are Kathleen Arbogast, Claudia Craig, Steve LeRoy, Debbie Lesko, Kathy Prager, Judith Shaffer, Robin Spence, Robert Sweet, Anne Walton, Judy Wikler and Janet Wunderlich.

We have a new point system for the honor roll. You get three points for an A, two for a B and one for a C. For a (C) and D you get nothing. Multiply this by the number of hours you spend in class and add. To get on the honor roll you need at least 70 points.

If you made the honor roll this time, do it again, and if you didn't, better luck next time.

Wedding Bells

On January 19, 1957, at 3:00 Miss Nancy Hirschbuhl married Richard W. Shepherd. The wedding took place at the Queen of Peace Church in Ardsley. She plans to continue working. She is now living in Glenside and likes married life very much.

On December 22, 1956, at 10:00 A.M. Miss Eileen Johnson married Joseph Ricci. The wedding took place at St. Rose of Lima in West Philadelphia. She also plans to continue teaching. She is now living in Willow Grove and likes married life very much.

Slick Six

On February 1, 1957, the girls' basketball team played Rockledge at Rockledge. This was the second time we played them and the second time the Ghosts beat them. The score of the varsity game was 23-20. The score of the junior varsity game was 43-2.

For more information please contact the

illustrator at info@suevanhook.com

Printed in the United States
by Baker & Taylor Publisher Services